Specials!

Food 2

Roy Ballam and Janet Wilson

Acknowledgements

Pg. 6, 36 (bottom) Crown copyright material is reproduced with the permission of the Controller Office of Public Sector Information (OPSI). Reproduced under the terms of the Click-Use Licence; pg. 18 tips quoted from the Food Standards Agency (www.eatwell.gov.uk/healthydiet/eighttipssection/8tips/); pg. 36 The Vegetarian Society, Parkdale, Altrincham, Cheshire, WA14 4QG. For a full listing of products and services approved by the Vegetarian Society, visit www.seedlingshowcase.com/corporate08/products.asp Tel: 0161 925 2000 (top left); The Soil Association organic symbol is a registered certification mark (®) of Soil Association Limited (top right); Red Tractor logo: Assured Food Standards, www.redtractor.org.uk (middle); © 2009 Fairtrade Foundation (middle right);

United Kingdom: Folens Publishers, Waterslade House, Thame Road, Haddenham, Buckinghamshire, HP17 8NT.
Email: folens@folens.com Website: www.folens.com

Ireland: Folens Publishers, Greenhills Road, Tallaght, Dublin 24.
Email: info@folens.ie Website: www.folens.ie

Commissioning editor: Paul Naish   Editor: Cathy Hurren

Text design and layout: Planman

Illustrator: Lee Nicholls/www.hardwickstudios.com; additional artwork: Julian Baker (JB Illustrations): pg. 8 (sausage roll, chips, yogurt); pg. 15 (lamb chop, yogurt); pg. 16 (child in wheelchair); pg. 24 (sieve, whisk, colander, spoon, grater); pg. 56 (tuna); pg. 57 (yogurt); pg. 57 (lettuce); Sarah Deakin/www.hardwickstudios.com: pg. 8 (crisps, can, carton, salad, curry); pg. 10 (can, carrots, pasta); pg. 15 (carrots, honey); pg. 18 (carrots); pg. 22 (fruit bowl, vegetables, pasta, chicken, bottle); pg. 24 (clock); pg. 26 (curry); pg. 30 (computer); pg. 31 (computer); pg. 36 (mobius loop); pg. 42 (salad, curry, computer); pg. 48 (cake); pg. 54 (vegetables, banana); pg. 55 (banana); pg. 57 (banana); pg. 61 (banana); Tony Randell: pg. 10 (cheese); pg. 15 (beefburger, cheese); pg. 37 (cheese)

Cover design: Holbrook Design   Cover image: © iStockphoto.com/DNY59

First published 2009 by Folens Limited.

Every effort has been made to contact copyright holders of material used in this publication. If any copyright holder has been overlooked, we will be pleased to make any necessary arrangements.

British Library Cataloguing in Publication Data. A catalogue record for this publication is available from the British Library.

ISBN 978-1-85008-463-1   Folens code FD4631

Contents

Introduction

Specials! Design and Technology activities are planned for students with a reading comprehension age of seven to nine years and working at levels 1 to 3. This book provides essential activities to help students apply and consolidate their learning in food technology with regards healthy eating, understanding the needs of others and consumer issues. It also supports students' understanding of the functional role of ingredients and being creative with food. Recipe challenges are included to help students set their learning in context and promote inspiring practical work.

This book contains ten separate units covering the topics needed to complete the theme of the book. Each unit has one or more photocopiable Resource sheets and several Activity sheets. This allows the teacher to work in different ways. The tasks are differentiated throughout the book and offer all students the opportunity to expand their skills.

The teacher can work in different ways: each unit could be taught as one or two lessons with students working individually, in pairs or in groups. Alternatively, a single Resource sheet and the related Activity sheet(s) could be used as required. Some student pages are more challenging than others so they will need to be selected accordingly.

The Teacher's notes give guidance and are laid out as follows:

Objectives
These are the main skills or knowledge to be learnt.

Prior knowledge
This refers to the minimum skills or knowledge required by students to complete the tasks. Some Activity sheets are more challenging than others and will need to be selected accordingly.

Links
All units link to the Design and Technology National Curriculum at Key Stage 3, Scottish attainment targets, and the Northern Ireland and Welsh Programmes of Study.

Background
This gives additional information for the teacher about particular aspects of the topic.

Starter activity
Since the units can be taught as a lesson, a warm-up activity focusing on an aspect of the unit is suggested.

Resource sheets and Activity sheets
The Resource sheets are used as stimulus for discussion and contain no tasks or activities. Where useful, keywords are given in the Teacher's notes and related tasks are provided on the Activity sheets. Links with other Activity sheets are sometimes indicated.

Plenary
The teacher can use the suggestions here to do additional work, recap on the main points covered, or reinforce a particular point.

Assessment sheet
At the end of the book there is an Assessment sheet focusing on student progress and learning. It can be used in different ways. A student could complete it as a self-assessment, while the teacher or support assistant also complete one on the student's progress. The two can then be compared and contrasted during a discussion. Alternatively, students could work in pairs to carry out a peer-assessment and then compare outcomes.

Look out for other titles in the Design and Technology series, including:
- Designing and making
- Food
- Graphic products
- Product design
- Resistant materials
- Sustainable design
- Systems and control
- Textiles
- Textiles 2

Teacher's notes

Healthy eating

Objectives

- To recognize and name the five food groups from *The eatwell plate*
- To apply the messages from *The eatwell plate* to their own and others' diets
- To match the food groups to their main nutrients

Prior knowledge

Students should be aware of the names of a range of foods and food groups. Some may also have an understanding of what constitutes a balanced diet.

NC links

Key concepts: 1.2 Cultural understanding; 1.4 Critical evaluation
Key processes: c, h
Range and content: a, b, c, d, h
Curriculum opportunities: a, g

Northern Ireland PoS

Home economics: Diet and health: a, b

Scottish attainment targets

Health education: Physical health: Level C

Welsh PoS

Skills: Designing: 2, 4
Skills: Making: 8, 9

Background

This unit covers the principles of healthy eating, as depicted by *The eatwell plate* – the UK model for healthy eating. The model shows the proportions and types of foods that comprise a healthy, balanced diet over a period of time. It is divided into five food groups. The key to a healthy lifestyle is a balanced and varied diet, combined with being active.

Starter activity

Ask students whether they could categorize foods into different groups. What would the groups be called? What foods would they contain? Record their ideas on the whiteboard. Manoeuvre the discussion towards the five food groups depicted by *The eatwell plate*.

Resource sheets and Activity sheets

Use the Resource sheet, 'The eatwell plate', to introduce students to the concept of *The eatwell plate*. Reinforce the fact that this is the UK model for healthy eating and that we do not use the food pyramid. *The eatwell plate* shows the proportions and the five food groups that we need to eat to maintain health. Although water and salt do not appear on the plate, it is important to drink plenty of water throughout the day and reduce an excessive intake of salt.

Using the Activity sheet, 'The food groups', students are to name foods from each of the five food groups shown on *The eatwell plate*. Students could be provided with samples of food from each of the groups to provoke a discussion and provide interest. Students should be encouraged to explain which food group's items should be eaten the least and why.

The Activity sheet, 'What is a balanced diet?', reinforces the main message from *The eatwell plate*. Students are required to compare two diets against *The eatwell plate* to identify any types of food that are missing as well as highlight proportion size. Students are then encouraged to provide suggestions as to how the diets could be changed to make them healthier.

Using the Activity sheet, 'Eat well for a day', students are required to keep a food diary for a day to log everything they eat and drink. They should then compare their diet against *The eatwell plate* and suggest changes they could make to ensure they are following a healthy diet.

Using the Activity sheet, 'Nutrition matters', discuss with students the five food groups and the nutrients that help to maintain health. In small groups or as a class, students should cut out the cards from the Activity sheet and match the food group to the main nutrients it provides. As an extension, students could investigate the functions of different nutrients.

Plenary

Ask students to create a list of at least eight healthy eating tips based on *The eatwell plate*.

The eatwell plate

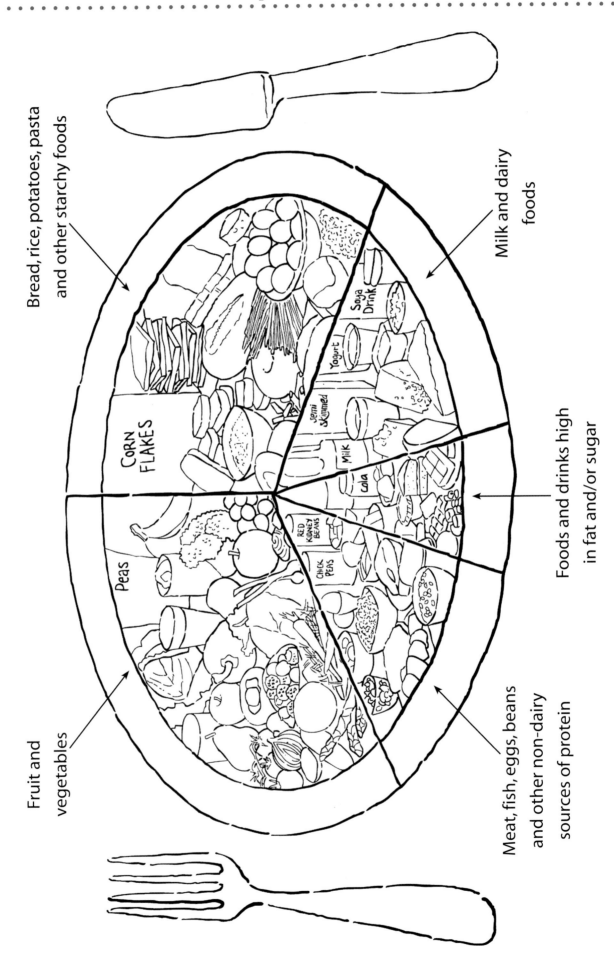

Bread, rice, potatoes, pasta and other starchy foods

Milk and dairy foods

Foods and drinks high in fat and/or sugar

Meat, fish, eggs, beans and other non-dairy sources of protein

Fruit and vegetables

CoRN FLAKES

Soya Drink

Yogurt

Semi Skimmed

Milk

Cola

Peas

RED KIDNEY BEANS

CHICK PEAS

Food 2

The food groups

☞ Name four foods that belong to each of the five food groups from *The eatwell plate*.

The eatwell plate food groups	Foods in the group
1 Fruit and vegetables	1 _____ 2 _____ 3 _____ 4 _____
2 Bread, rice, potatoes, pasta and other starchy foods	1 _____ 2 _____ 3 _____ 4 _____
3 Milk and dairy foods	1 _____ 2 _____ 3 _____ 4 _____
4 Meat, fish, eggs, beans and other non-dairy sources of protein	1 _____ 2 _____ 3 _____ 4 _____
5 Foods and drinks high in fat and/or sugar	1 _____ 2 _____ 3 _____ 4 _____

Activity sheet – Healthy eating

What is a balanced diet?

To achieve a balanced diet we all need to eat the right types and amounts of different foods. *The eatwell plate* shows the right types and amounts of different foods that we need to eat to stay healthy.

☞ 1 Study the following diets for two different people.

A 14-year-old teenager

A 28-year-old woman

Breakfast
Packet of crisps
Can of lemonade

Snack
Blueberry muffin

Lunch
Sausage roll
Chocolate bar
Yogurt

Dinner
Spaghetti Bolognese
Chips
Strawberry mousse

Breakfast
Fruit salad
Orange juice

Snack
Grapes
Grapefruit juice

Lunch
Salad
Apple juice

Dinner
Vegetable curry with rice
Apple

☞ 2 Compare these two diets with *The eatwell plate*. Answer the following questions:

- Are any of the food groups missing?
- Are the correct proportions being eaten?
- How could the diets be more balanced?

Activity sheet – Healthy eating

Eat well for a day

To see if your diet is healthy and balanced, keep a food diary for a day.

☞ 1 For each meal, colour in the food group of *The eatwell plate* that you have eaten. List all of the food and drink you had for that meal.

Meal	Food and drink consumed
Breakfast	
Snacks	
Lunch	
Dinner	

☞ 2 Compare your diary to *The eatwell plate* and complete the paragraph below.

   My diary shows that _____

   _____ .

   I have consumed food and drink from _____ *of the five food groups.*

☞ 3 Write down what changes you could make to make your diet more healthy and balanced. _____

   _____

   _____

Nutrition matters

Different types of foods provide different nutrients that the body needs to function well. It is important to eat a variety and a balance of foods to stay healthy.

☞ 1 Cut out the cards below. They show the five food groups, different types of food and a range of nutrients.

Fruit and vegetables	Minced beef	Baked beans	Calcium
Bread, rice, potatoes, pasta and other starchy foods	Milk	Cheese	Fat Carbohydrate (sugar)
Milk and dairy foods	Oil	Can of lemonade	Protein Iron
Meat, fish, eggs, beans and other non-dairy sources of protein	Oranges	Carrots	Carbohydrate Fibre
Foods and drinks high in fat and/or sugar	Bread	Pasta	Vitamin A Vitamin C

☞ 2 Match the food group to the food items and the nutrients that those foods provide.

☞ 3 Explain the functions of the nutrients listed above. Use the following keywords to help you:

- Energy
- Growth
- Repair
- Healthy
- Bones
- Teeth
- Eyes
- Skin
- Gut
- Blood

Teacher's notes

The needs of people

Objectives

- To understand that a range of factors can determine what people eat
- To consider the food needs of other people
- To list factors that affect their own food choices

Prior knowledge

Some students will be aware of particular food needs if, for example, they have experience of an issue such as an allergy. Students should recognize that they consume different food and drink, and that there are a number of factors that affect their food choices.

NC links

Key concepts: 1.2 Cultural understanding; 1.4 Critical evaluation
Key processes: c, h
Range and content: a, b, c, d, h
Curriculum opportunities: a, g

Northern Ireland PoS

Home economics: Diet and health: a, b

Scottish attainment targets

Health education: Physical health: Level C
Technology: Needs and how they are met: Level C
Developing informed attitudes: Respect and care for self and others, Social and environmental responsibility

Welsh PoS

Skills: Designing: 2, 4, 8
Skills: Making: 8

Background

The food and drink we consume is determined by a range of factors, some of which are beyond our control. Diets vary between individuals for reasons such as food availability, preference, money, resources, time, culture and religion. In addition, factors such as allergies, ethical beliefs or peer pressure also impact on choices made.

Starter activity

Ask students to discuss the question: why do we eat different types of food? Record their answers on the whiteboard. Discuss with students which of these factors they control and which factors are beyond their control.

Resource sheets and Activity sheets

The Resource sheet, 'Needs and wants', highlights to students some of the essential reasons why we need food, as well as reasons why we might want certain types of food. This sheet could form the basis of a class discussion: what do students think are needs and wants? What do they believe is the difference? Challenge students to write about additional needs and wants.

The Activity sheet, 'Diet through life', encourages students to think about the different food needs people have during different stages of their life. This activity could be done in small groups or as a whole class. This task could be extended by asking students to look at the needs of a particular life stage in detail.

The Activity sheet, 'Factors affecting food choices', requires students to list different factors that affect what they eat. In small groups or as a class, students should discuss the factors that they have listed and discuss if they are different or similar to each other.

The Activity sheet, 'Vegans and vegetarians', explains the concept of veganism and vegetarianism and requires students to identify what they do and do not eat. If there are some students who are already vegan or vegetarian, encourage them to explain their choice to the class.

The Activity sheet, 'Allergies', explains to students some types of food allergies or intolerances that people can have. Some people have an allergy or intolerance to certain ingredients. If they eat foods to which they are allergic, they can become ill. Students are required to decide which foods from a menu guests with different allergies or intolerances could choose. This task could be extended by encouraging students to change the menu to better suit the needs of the guests.

Plenary

Students could cook (and/or modify) a range of dishes suitable for the needs of different people.

Needs and wants

Activity sheet – The needs of people

Diet through life

We all need different types and amounts of food during different stages of our lives. For example, a baby's needs are different to a teenager's needs. Our bodies require different amounts of energy and nutrients to grow and maintain health.

☞ 1 Cut out the cards below.

 A baby boy	Energy and nutrient requirements continue to increase as they grow. Daily energy used: 8240 kJ (1970 kcal)
 A toddler	Additional energy and nutrient requirements are needed to support the baby's development. Daily energy used: 8900 kJ (2127 kcal)
 A teenager	Breast milk is ideal. It helps support a baby's early development and growth. Daily energy used: 2280 kJ (545 kcal)
 An adult	Maintain a good bodyweight, for height. No further growth is expected. Daily energy used: 10600 kJ (2550 kcal)
 A pregnant woman	A period of rapid growth, development and change. Mineral intake, such as iron, is very important. Daily energy used: 8830 kJ (2110 kcal)

☞ 2 Match each person to the correct life stage that identifies their needs.

Activity sheet – The needs of people

Factors affecting food choices

Why do we eat the foods we do? Everyone eats different types of foods for a number of different reasons. These are known as **factors**.

☞ 1 Stick a photo of yourself in the space below or draw a self-portrait.

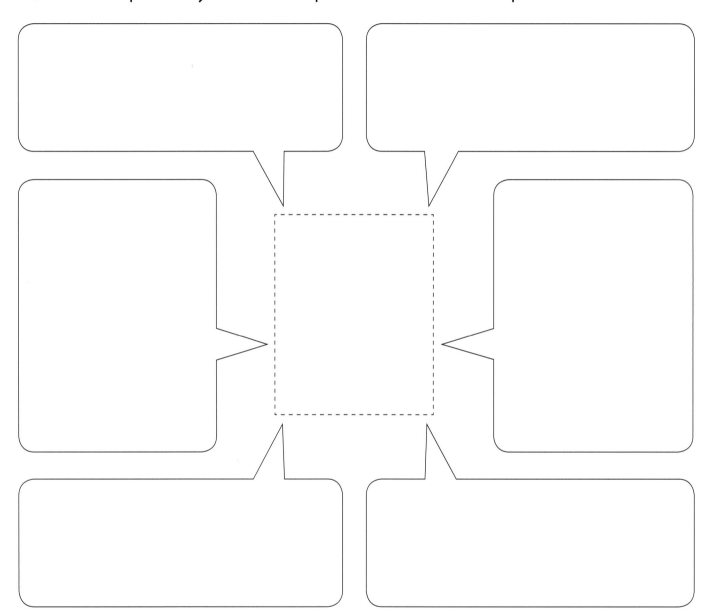

☞ 2 Think about the food that you eat. List the different **factors** that affect what you eat. Explain your answers. Use the word bank to help.

Word bank

- Time of day
- Preference
- Likes/dislikes
- Shops
- Friends
- Religion
- Culture
- Cost
- Special occasions

Activity sheet – The needs of people

Vegans and vegetarians

Some people choose not to eat certain foods, for moral, religious or health reasons. For example, vegetarians do not eat meat or fish. Vegans do not eat meat, fish or foods produced by an animal such as dairy foods or honey.

☞ Draw arrows from each of the foods shown to match what can be eaten by a vegan or vegetarian.

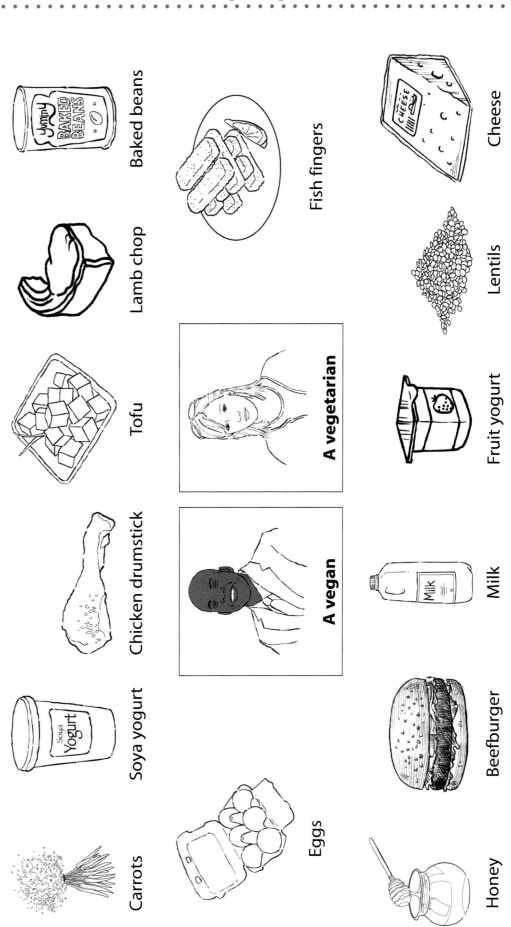

Baked beans

Lamb chop

Fish fingers

Cheese

Tofu

Lentils

A vegetarian

Fruit yogurt

Chicken drumstick

A vegan

Milk

Soya yogurt

Carrots

Eggs

Beefburger

Honey

Activity sheet – The needs of people

Allergies

Some people have a food allergy or intolerance. This means that they could become ill if they eat certain ingredients or foods to which they are allergic. People with food allergies need to be careful when they eat out. Some allergies and intolerances include:

- Egg
- Milk
- Nut
- Shellfish
- Wheat
- Peanut

The following six friends are visiting a restaurant for dinner. They each have a food allergy or intolerance.

No egg.

No milk or other dairy products.

No nuts.

No peanuts.

☞ 1 Study the menu below.

Menu

Starters
Prawn cocktail

Walnut, apple and lettuce salad

Roasted vegetable soup

Mains
Bacon quiche

Stir-fry chicken with rice or noodles

Vegetable stuffed peppers with cheese topping

Desserts
Peanut brownie

Banana and custard

Fresh fruit salad

No shellfish.

No wheat.

☞ 2 In your workbook, write down which dishes each person could order.

☞ 3 How could the menu be changed to better meet the needs of one of the six friends?

Food 2   © Folens (copiable page)

Teacher's notes

Food for life

Objectives

- To link the requirements of different foods (nutrients) to different health issues
- To understand the concept of energy balance and the consequences of negative and positive energy balance
- To produce a list of tips for an active lifestyle based around diet and activity

Prior knowledge

Students should know about *The eatwell plate* and the nutrients provided by different foods.

NC links

Key concepts: 1.2 Cultural understanding; 1.4 Critical evaluation
Key processes: c, h
Range and content: a, b, c, d, e, h
Curriculum opportunities: a, g

Northern Ireland PoS

Home economics: Diet and health: a, b

Scottish attainment targets

Health education: Physical health: Level B
Developing informed attitudes: Respect and care for self and others

Welsh PoS

Skills: Designing: 2, 4
Skills: Making: 8, 9

Background

Different foods provide different essential nutrients that keep us fit and healthy. If we do not eat the right types of foods we may not get enough of certain nutrients, which can lead to health problems both now and in the future. Students may find it difficult to appreciate future health problems, such as heart disease, but some issues can be more immediate and gain their attention, for example, the thought of maintaining healthy teeth and skin.

Starter activity

Write the following words on the whiteboard: obesity, heart disease, bone health, healthy teeth. Ask students to suggest other words they associate with those written on the board. Seek to link the health issues with diet, activity and potential solutions to promote positive health.

Resource sheets and Activity sheets

The Resource sheet, 'Food for life', provides a montage of different aspects of health to be used as a way of generating a class discussion. Ask students to identify the different health issues illustrated on the sheet and suggest other health issues that could be included. Students could be encouraged to suggest which foods and nutrients link to different health issues.

The Activity sheet, 'Food and health', requires students to work out which food and nutrients link to different health issues. This can help to reinforce issues looked at using the Resource sheet, 'Food for life'.

The Activity sheet, 'Health issues', highlights to students the seriousness of diets that are high in saturated fat, salt and sugar, which can lead to heart disease, hypertension and dental issues. Students should be encouraged to look at ways in which these foods can realistically be reduced in a person's diet. This task could be extended by asking students to modify and cook a range of recipes to consolidate the teaching points.

The Activity sheet, 'Energy balance', explains the concept of attaining energy balance – the energy provided by the food and drink we consume equals what we use through being physically active. A see-saw is used to illustrate this concept. Students should consider the two case studies provided and suggest what might happen to the energy balance over a period of time. This task could be extended by students keeping a diary of their food intake and any physical activity they take part in to see if they are in energy balance.

The Activity sheet, 'Maintaining a healthy lifestyle', requires students to write six tips about diet and exercise that others could follow. This sheet emphasises that eating a variety and a balance of foods, as well as being active, are vital for a healthy lifestyle.

Plenary

Students could extend the task on the Activity sheet, 'Maintaining a healthy lifestyle', by using their tips as pledges for a class display. Students could revisit their pledges a few months later to see if they've kept to their own tips!

Food for life

ENERGY BALANCE
ENERGY BALANCE
ENERGY BALANCE
ENERGY BALANCE
ENERGY BALANCE

ENERGY
BALANCE

Strong
bones **Strong**
Strong **Strong** **bones**
Strong bones
Strong
bones
Strong
bones
Strong
bones

Strong
bones

Healthy teeth
Healthy teeth
Healthy teeth
Healthy teeth

Strong
bones
Strong
bones
Strong
bones

Strong
bones

Eight tips for eating well

1 Base your meals on starchy foods

2 Eat lots of fruit and veg

3 Eat more fish

4 Cut down on saturated fat and sugar

5 Try to eat less salt – no more than 6g a day

6 Get active and try to be a healthy weight

7 Drink plenty of water

8 Don't skip breakfast

Food 2

Food and health

'You are what you eat' is a common saying. Different foods provide different nutrients that keep us fit and healthy. If we do not eat the right types of foods we may not get enough nutrients. This can lead to health problems both now and in the future.

☞ 1 Below are the health reasons why we need to eat certain types of food. Fill in the missing words.

Food	Nutrients	Health reasons
O_____	V_____ _____	Healthy skin
C_____	V_____ _____	N_____ _____
W_____ bread	_____	G_____ health
Yogurt	C_____	S_____ b_____
B_____	I_____	H_____ b_____

☞ 2 Below are the health reasons why we need to eat less of certain foods, or change them to make them healthier. Fill in the missing words.

Food	Eat less...	Health reasons
_____	Sugar	_____ teeth
Ready-made pizza	S_____	High blood pressure
Fried samosa	_____	Ob_____

Word bank

- Calcium
- Orange
- Healthy
- Carrots
- Wholemeal
- Iron
- Healthy blood
- Vitamin A
- Sweets
- Obesity
- Strong bones
- Fat
- Vitamin C
- Salt
- Fibre
- Beef
- Gut
- Night vision

Health issues

It is a good idea to keep the amount of fat, sugar and salt you eat in check. Many people's diets are high in fat, sugar and salt which can lead to serious health problems. For example:

- Eating too many foods high in fat can lead to heart disease
- Eating too many sugary foods between meals can lead to dental caries
- Eating too much salt can result in high blood pressure.

What you eat can affect your life both now and in the future. Making simple changes to the types of food, or the way in which it is prepared or cooked, can make all the difference.

☞ Suggest three ways of cutting down on fat, sugar and salt. Think about alternative options of the same foods, the preparation and the cooking method. Use the ideas bank to help you.

Cutting down on fat	Cutting down on sugar	Cutting down on salt
1	1	1
2	2	2
3	3	3

Ideas bank

- Trim the fat off meat
- Currant bun
- Grill
- Remove the skin
- Canned in juice/water

- Herbs and spices
- Reduced fat
- Grate
- Steam
- Fruit juice

- Sugar-free
- Fruit
- Low salt
- Low fat

Activity sheet – Food for life

Energy balance

To maintain a healthy weight you need to ensure that the energy you take in (food) equals the energy you use (activity). This is called being in **energy balance**. The see-saw on the right shows energy balance.

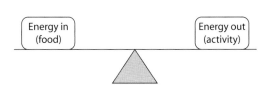

☞ 1 Study the see-saws below for two different people.

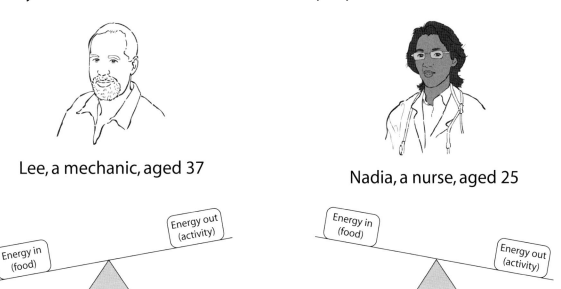

Lee, a mechanic, aged 37

Nadia, a nurse, aged 25

☞ 2 Answer the following questions about Lee.

a Is Lee in energy balance? _____

b What does the see-saw show? _____

c What will happen to Lee over time? _____

d What advice would you give to Lee? _____

_____

☞ 3 Answer the following questions about Nadia.

a Is Nadia in energy balance? _____

b What does the see-saw show? _____

c What will happen to Nadia over time? _____

d What advice would you give to Nadia? _____

_____

Maintaining a healthy lifestyle

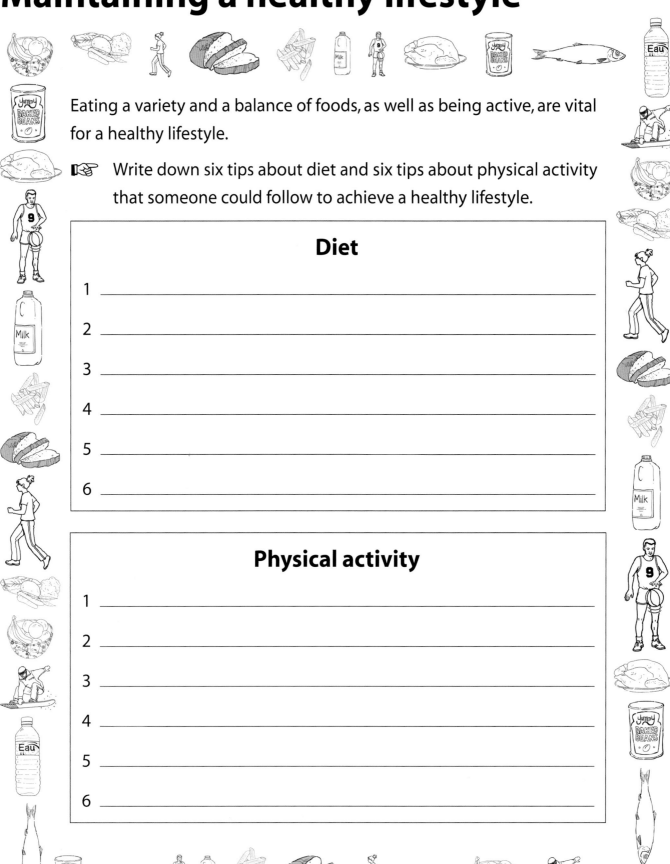

Eating a variety and a balance of foods, as well as being active, are vital for a healthy lifestyle.

☞ Write down six tips about diet and six tips about physical activity that someone could follow to achieve a healthy lifestyle.

Diet

1 _____
2 _____
3 _____
4 _____
5 _____
6 _____

Physical activity

1 _____
2 _____
3 _____
4 _____
5 _____
6 _____

Food 2

Teacher's notes

Cooking for life

Objectives

- To plan meals based on the needs of others
- To identify ingredients from other countries
- To be creative when cooking, as well as be mindful of money
- To understand the advantages and disadvantages of convenience food products

Prior knowledge

Students will have different experiences of cooking, as well as an appreciation of different factors that affect what and how we cook. Students will also have experience of the food needs of others.

NC links

Key concepts: 1.1 Designing and making;
1.2 Cultural understanding
Key processes: b, c, d
Range and content: a, b, d, e, h
Curriculum opportunities: a, b, c

Northern Ireland PoS

Home economics: Diet and health: a, b;
Choice and management of resources: a

Scottish attainment targets

Technology: Preparing for tasks: Level C

Welsh PoS

Skills: Designing: 2, 4, 8
Skills: Making: 8

Background

This unit reviews the different factors that influence how and what we prepare, cook and eat. Aspects of this will be subjective, using students' experiences and opinions to shape discussion and debate, for example, the use of convenience food products. Other aspects will be based on research of food customs of different countries and cultures.

Starter activity

Using a map of the world as a stimulus, ask students to describe ingredients, recipes or dishes that originate from a range of different countries. Discuss whether the ingredients, recipes and dishes are only available in that country or if they can also be purchased in the UK. This could be extended using the Activity sheet, 'Cultural shift'.

Resource sheets and Activity sheets

Using the Resource sheet, 'Cooking', discuss with students issues that could affect what and how they cook. They could work in small groups to focus and report back on one or two particular aspects listed on the sheet.

Using the Activity sheet, 'Meals for life', students are to consider the food needs of others by planning meals for three different groups of people. As a class, talk through different aspects that can influence food choices throughout life. It might be useful to have a selection of recipe books and/or access to the Internet to research recipes. This activity could be extended by students cooking some of the dishes they suggest.

Using the Activity sheet, 'Cultural shift', discuss with students the vast range of ingredients, recipes and dishes that are available from around the world. Introduce them to the concept of fusion foods (a food dish that has been influenced by two or more different food cultures, for example, a Yorkshire pudding with a curry filling). Students are encouraged to list ingredients from four different countries and use them to produce some fusion food ideas.

The Activity sheet, 'Credit crunch', focuses on the use of leftover food when cooking. It is highlighted to students that using leftovers saves money and reduces waste. Students are encouraged to suggest ways in which leftovers can be used to create new dishes. Remind them that leftovers should be eaten the next day or frozen and used within a month. This activity could be extended by students calculating the cost of their ingredients/dishes.

The Activity sheet, 'Make it quick', requires students to explore the use of ready-made food components, such as jars of sauce and prepared vegetables. As a class, discuss the advantages and disadvantages of this type of food product.

Plenary

As a class, discuss how the work from this unit could be used when they plan and cook food products or dishes for other people. Encourage students to identify which important aspects they should consider.

Cooking

What affects how and what you cook?

Cooking skills

Ingredients and equipment

The occasion

Money

The time of day/time available

Tradition and culture

Healthy eating

Experience and age

Food 2

Activity sheet – Cooking for life

Meals for life

Throughout life our food needs change. Aspects that influence these changes are:

- Age
- Cost
- Likes and dislikes
- Healthy eating
- Appearance, taste and texture
- The occasion

☞ 1 Study the following three groups and decide what meal you would make for each. Give reasons for your choices.

Group	Meal	Reasons for choice
A party for a group of seven-year-old children		
A night in watching television with friends		
A group of retired people having a meal together		

☞ 2 What do you think makes a good meal?

_____

_____

_____

Activity sheet – Cooking for life

Culture shift

In the past, if you wanted to eat food from another country, you would have to arrange a visit! Today we use a range of ingredients and dishes from around the world. Sometimes these are combined to create **fusion foods**.

☞ 1 List four ingredients that come from four different countries. An example has been given to help you.

Country 1 _Italy_	Country 2	Country 3	Country 4
Parmesan cheese			

☞ 2 Using some of the ingredients you have listed, create fusion dishes for the foods below.

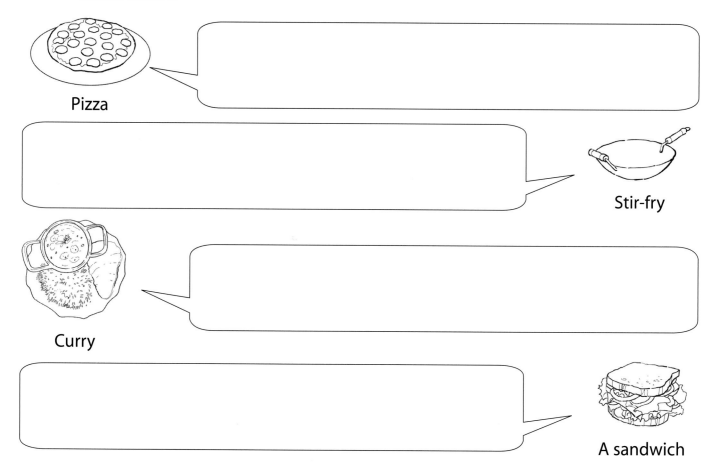

Pizza

Stir-fry

Curry

A sandwich

Food 2

Activity sheet – Cooking for life

Credit crunch

When money is tight, being a creative cook in the kitchen can help to save pennies. Leftovers from a meal are often thrown away. But stop! Leftovers can be used again the next day to help save money and reduce food waste.

☞ What could you make from the leftovers below?

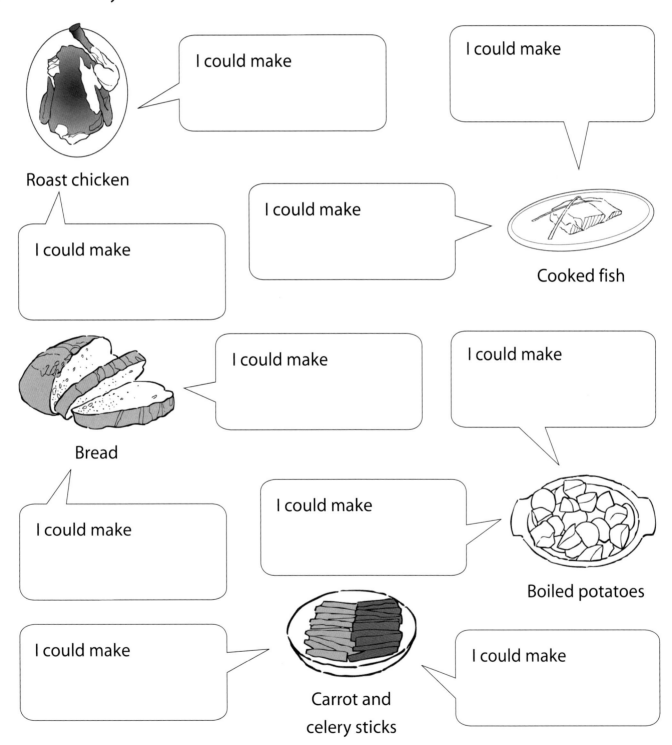

Roast chicken

I could make

I could make

I could make

I could make

Cooked fish

Bread

I could make

I could make

I could make

I could make

Boiled potatoes

I could make

Carrot and celery sticks

I could make

Make it quick

When you cook at home, you might do some of the following:

Reheat a ready-meal, such as a frozen lasagne or pizza.	Use ready-made components, such as a jar of sauce or a bag of stir-fry vegetables	Prepare and cook a dish from scratch, such as soup.

☞ 1 Ready-meals and ready-made components are popular. Name two advantages and two disadvantages of using these types of foods.

Advantages	Disadvantages
1	1
2	2

Djamel has friends coming round to watch television. He plans to cook chicken stir-fry. Time has run out and he can't make it from scratch.

☞ 2 What ready-made components could Djamel use to save time?

Ingredients	
● Raw chicken pieces →	
● Vegetables: pak choi, bean sprouts, carrots, red pepper, mushrooms →	
● Dried noodles →	
For the sauce ● soy, oil, fresh ginger, garlic, red chilli →	

Teacher's notes

Wise food shopping

Objectives

- To recognize and identify a range of food shops
- To choose foods that meet specific needs
- To have an awareness of value for money when shopping

Prior knowledge

Students should be aware of the role of shops. Shops source and purchase processed and unprocessed foods, store, display and sell them to the public. Shops have to cover the cost of their overheads and make a profit to stay in business.

NC links

Key concepts: 1.1 Designing and making
Key processes: c, d, f, h
Range and content: a
Curriculum opportunities: a

Northern Ireland PoS

Home economics: Choice and management of resources: a, b, d

Scottish attainment targets

Technology: Needs and how they are met: Level A
Resources and how they are managed: Level A

Welsh PoS

Designing skills: 2
Making skills: 1, 2, 6, 7

Background

This unit will help develop students' knowledge and understanding of where to shop, what to buy, writing a shopping list and making suitable choices by considering the relative cost of food. Conducting shopping trips or allowing students access to Internet shopping sites will help reinforce learning.

Starter activity

Show students some bread, fresh fruit and a can of tuna. Ask them to identify which shops these items can be bought from. Discuss the variety of foods sold in supermarkets and in specialist food shops. Ask students if their families grow their own fruit and vegetables, make bread or go fishing as an alternative means of obtaining food.

Resource sheets and Activity sheets

The Resource sheet, 'Where do we shop?', introduces students to a range of different types of food shop. As a class, discuss which shops they are familiar with; students should include ideas of the own. If possible, visit a supermarket and a specialist shop so students can appreciate the range of products each shop sells, the relative size of the shops, facilities they provide, staff expertise and possible comparative costs.

The Activity sheet, 'Questionnaire: where do you shop?', asks students to extend their awareness of where their peers frequently or rarely shop by conducting a questionnaire. Answers can be recorded as a bar chart, but if computers are available, students could be encouraged to present their findings as a graph using ICT.

The Activity sheet, 'Shopping lists', encourages students to identify items already in a store cupboard and fridge in order to create shopping lists for specific meals. This could be carried out as a practical exercise, with varying examples of food items and meals.

The Activity sheet, 'Making the right choice', aims to raise students' awareness of the range of choices available in relation to one food item available in many shops. Cheese is used as the example. A class visit to a cheese shop, a cheese counter in a supermarket or a cheese tasting session would enhance this task for students.

The Activity sheet, 'Value for money', gives students the opportunity to consider ingredients required to make coleslaw, to make it, and to compare the cost of a home-made version and a ready-made version. Students are encouraged to consider the fact that the ingredients required to make something cannot always be bought in the quantities specified. As a class, discuss the advantages and disadvantages of both home-made and ready-made products.

Plenary

Discuss with students if their experiences from this unit have changed where they would shop.

Resource sheet – Wise food shopping

Where do we shop?

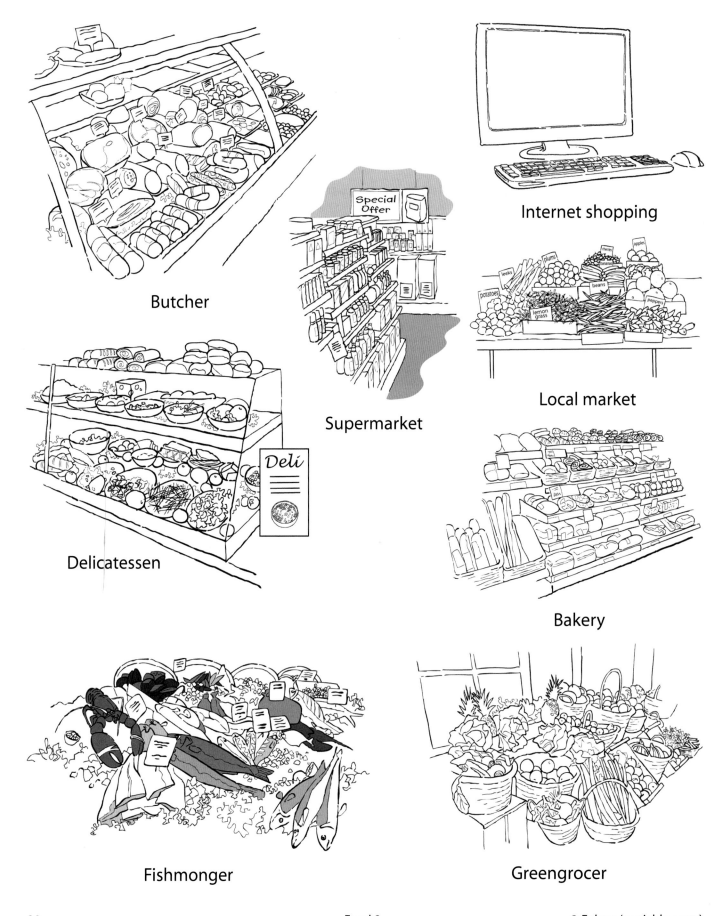

Butcher

Supermarket

Internet shopping

Local market

Delicatessen

Bakery

Fishmonger

Greengrocer

Activity sheet – Wise food shopping

Questionnaire: where do you shop?

☞ 1 Ask five people the following questions and record their answers.

Where do you buy your food from?		
	Yes, often	No, rarely
A supermarket		
A local market		
A delicatessen		
Local shops: a butcher, a greengrocer, a bakery, a fishmonger		
Internet shopping		
Other places, for example, farmers' market, Asian or oriental food shop		

☞ 2 Present your results to show the most popular types of shop and the number of people that shop there. You could do this as a graph.

Activity sheet – Wise food shopping

Shopping lists

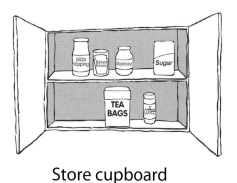

Store cupboard

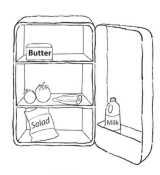

Fridge

☞ Check the food stored in the cupboard and the fridge. Write two shopping lists for the ingredients you need to buy to the make the two meals shown below.

Meal 1	Meal 2
Baked potato with tuna mayonnaise, a salad, a glass of orange juice and a yogurt for dessert.	Pepperoni pizza with a cup of tea and a bunch of grapes for dessert.
Shopping list	**Shopping list**

Word bank

- Baking potato
- Pizza base
- Mozzarella cheese
- Pepperoni
- Orange juice
- Grapes
- Yogurt
- Tuna

Activity sheet – Wise food shopping

Making the right choice

There can be a lot of different choices available when you shop, even for just one food item!

☞ All of these shoppers want to buy some cheese. Suggest which type of cheese they should buy. Draw arrows to the cheese or cheeses. The first one has been done for you.

I am going to make a cheesecake.

Cheddar cheese slices

I like cheese spread on my toast.

Half-fat cheese

I have been advised to follow a low-fat diet.

Cream cheese

I don't have much time but want to make a cheese and tomato sandwich.

Cheese spread

I try to eat food produced with no pesticides.

Blue cheese

I am going to make a cheese sauce.

Organic cheese

I need cheese to eat with biscuits at my dinner party.

Farmhouse mature cheese

Food 2

Activity sheet – Wise food shopping

Value for money

You want some coleslaw to eat with a baked potato. You have decided to compare a ready-made pot of coleslaw with a home-made version.

☞ 1 Shop for the following items and write down what you paid for each one.

Shopping list

- 100g tub of low-fat coleslaw   £ _____
- ½ small white cabbage   £ _____
- 2 small carrots   £ _____
- ½ small red onion   £ _____
- 200g low-fat mayonnaise   £ _____

☞ 2 Make home-made coleslaw:

    1   Finely slice the cabbage and the onion.

    2   Grate the carrots and add to the cabbage and onion.

    3   Add the mayonnaise and mix together.

☞ 3 Compare the cost of the ready-made pot of coleslaw with your home-made version. Use the calculation below to work out how much 100g of your home-made coleslaw costs.

$$\text{Cost of 100g} = \frac{\text{Total cost of ingredients} \quad £ \_\_\_\_\_}{\text{Total weight in grams} \quad \_\_\_\_\_} \times 100$$

£ _____

☞ 4 Answer the following questions:

    a Which coleslaw was the cheapest for 100g? _____

    b Which coleslaw tasted the best? _____

    c Which would you eat and why? _____

Teacher's notes

Consumer awareness

Objectives

- To be able to name and locate foods from the UK
- To be more aware, and make use of, the information on food packaging
- To understand seasonal foods and make use of them when in season

Prior knowledge

Depending on where students live they may have some understanding of food that is grown, reared or produced locally. Students should be familiar with food packaging. Students should also be familiar with the seasons and may have already experienced growing or picking fruit and vegetables at particular times of the year.

NC links

Key concepts: 1.1 Designing and making;
1.2 Cultural understanding; 1.4 Critical evaluation
Key processes: c, d, f, g, h
Range and content: a, b, c, d, e, i
Curriculum opportunities: a, b, g

Northern Ireland PoS

Home economics: Diet and health: a, b, c;
Choice and management of resources: b, c

Scottish attainment targets

Health education: Physical health: Level C
Technology: Resources and how they are managed:
Level B
Developing informed attitudes: Respect and care for self and others

Welsh PoS

Skills: Designing: 2, 4, 8
Skills: Making: 5, 8

Background

An aspect of understanding food is linked to being an informed consumer. Being informed about the production and processing of food allows a consumer to make good choices for themselves and their family. In addition, how and where the food is produced may influence whether someone wishes to buy it. This could be due to ethical, environmental or financial considerations.

Starter activity

Introduce the term 'consumer awareness' to students. Lead a class discussion about what they think this means.

Resource sheets and Activity sheets

The Resource sheet, 'Do you know your food?', provides examples of a number of different symbols that appear on food packaging. As a class, ask students to identify each symbol and discuss which ones they have seen before. Explain to students that these symbols have been designed to help consumers make decisions about what food they buy. The symbols on the sheet include: the Red Tractor logo, the Soil Association logo, the Vegetarian Society Approved logo, the mobius loop, a gluten free symbol, the FAIRTRADE Mark, a GDA food label example and an example of the FSA traffic light label.

The Activity sheet, 'Origins of food', challenges students to match foods to their origin in the UK. As many people are now concerned about how far their food travels, this sheet helps to show students that a lot of food is grown, reared and produced in the UK. This activity could be extended by students thinking of food ideas of their own or by thinking up recipes using regional produce.

The Activity sheet, 'Food labels', encourages students to consider what information is put on to food packaging. You may wish to provide a display of food packaging to act as a stimulus. This activity could be extended by students identifying what kind of information on different examples of food packaging helps consumers to make their choices, for example, low-fat options.

The Activity sheet, 'A sign of good health?', highlights to students front of pack labelling. These labels help consumers make quick choices. Students are to evaluate the usefulness of both types of labelling.

The Activity sheet, 'Seasonal foods', requires students to think about what foods naturally grow when. Discuss with them the uses of seasonal foods, especially the preservation of fruit and vegetable glut, by freezing, pickling, and jam and chutney making for example.

Plenary

This work could be enhanced by planning cooking activities based around seasonal and local foods. In addition, samples of food packaging could be used to get students to compare products and become more familiar with different aspects of labelling information.

Do you know your food?

www.vegsoc.org

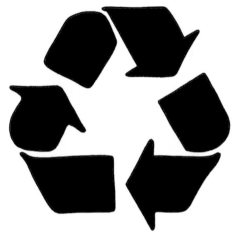

FAIRTRADE

Each portion contains:

Calories	Sugars	Fat	Saturates	Salt
218	6.3g	3.2g	1.4g	0.2g
11%	7%	5%	7%	3%

of an adult's guideline daily amount

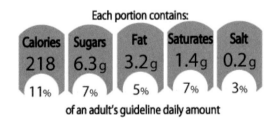

LOW Fat	LOW Sat Fat	HIGH Sugars	MED Salt
7.7g Per Serve	2.0g Per Serve	42.2g Per Serve	2.0g Per Serve

Activity sheet – Consumer awareness

Origins of food

Many people like to know where their food comes from. Some people are concerned with how far their food travels. Others want to know if it is locally produced.

☞ Draw arrows to show where the following food items come from in the UK.

Welsh rarebit

Cheddar cheese

Shortbread

Haggis

Chelsea bun

Irish stew

Welsh lamb

Leeks

Bara brith

Kent strawberries

Caerphilly cheese

Cornish pasty

Soda bread

Food labels

Activity sheet – Consumer awareness

Labels on food packaging provide important information to help us make choices.

☞ Fill in the gaps to complete the information that should appear on food packaging. Use the word bank to help you.

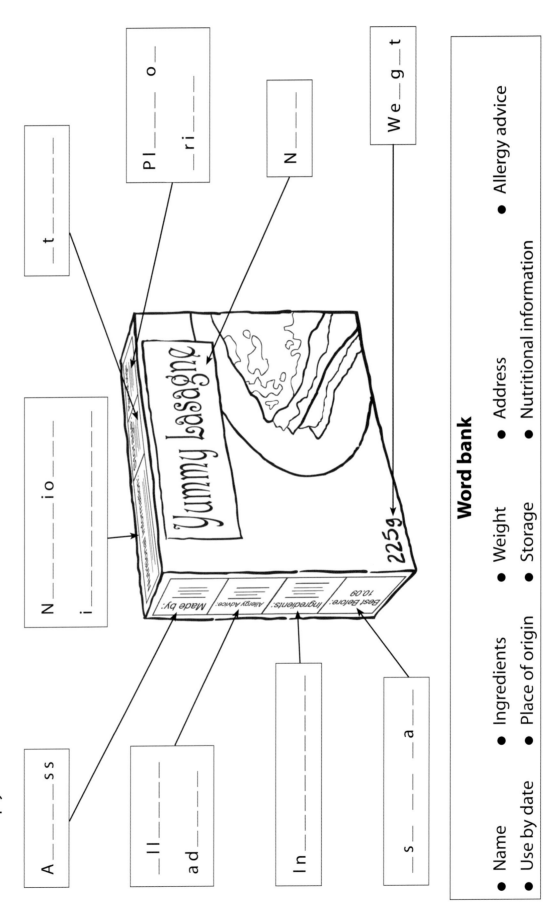

t _ _ _ _ _

Pl _ _ _ _ _ o _
_ _ _ ri _

N _ _ _ _

We _ g _ _ t

N _ _ _ _ io _ _ _ _
i _ _ _ _ _ _ _ _ _ _

A _ _ _ _ s s

ll _ _ _ _ _
a d _ _ _ _

In _ _ _ _ _ _ _ _ _

s _ _ _ a _ _

2259

Yummy Lasagne

Made by:
Allergy advice:
Ingredients:
Best Before: 10.09

Word bank

- Name
- Use by date
- Ingredients
- Place of origin
- Weight
- Storage
- Address
- Nutritional information
- Allergy advice

Activity sheet – Consumer awareness

A sign of good health?

Many food labels provide nutritional information. This information helps us to compare and choose between similar foods. This is to help us make quick and easy choices.

There are two main types of food labels for nutritional information:

Traffic light labels	**Guideline daily amounts (GDA)**
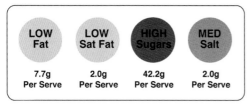	
The traffic light label shows the amount of fat, saturates, sugar and salt in a product by using colours.	The GDA label shows the percentage of calories, sugars, fat, saturates and salt in each serving, compared to the average needs of an adult.

- Green means there is a low amount, so is a healthier choice.
- Amber means there is a medium amount, so is OK to eat sometimes.
- Red means there is a high amount, so should only be eaten occasionally as a treat.

☞ 1 Do you think nutritional information is useful? Why? _____

_____

_____

☞ 2 Which of the two food labelling systems do you prefer? Why? _____

_____

_____

☞ 3 What do you think are the advantages and disadvantages of these two food labelling systems? _____

_____

_____

☞ 4 Collect examples of nutritional information from packaging and create a display.

Activity sheet – Consumer awareness

Seasonal foods

Many of the foods we buy are grown or reared during different seasons. We can buy food that is out of season because it is grown in greenhouses, or abroad, and imported to the UK.

☞ 1 Cut out the following picture cards. Place them in the correct season box.

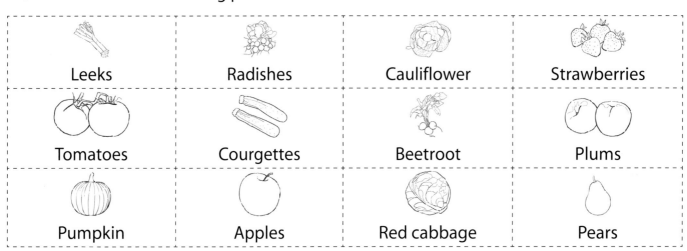

Leeks	Radishes	Cauliflower	Strawberries
Tomatoes	Courgettes	Beetroot	Plums
Pumpkin	Apples	Red cabbage	Pears

Winter	Spring

Summer	Autumn

☞ 2 Develop a meal idea for each season.

Teacher's notes

Creativity

Objectives

- To develop creativity when designing food dishes and products
- To use a number of appropriate methods of designing with food
- To generate ideas quickly and efficiently

Prior knowledge

Some students will have a broader background and experience of food, which will help their creativity. Others will require additional support, promoted through the use of engaging visual aids, sensory testing and cooking experiences. Use students' personal experiences of food to help them be creative.

NC links

Key concepts: 1.1 Designing and making; 1.2 Cultural understanding; 1.3 Creativity; 1.4 Critical evaluation
Key processes: a, b, c, d, h
Range and content: a, c
Curriculum opportunities: c

Northern Ireland PoS

Technology and design: Designing: a, b, c, d, e

Scottish attainment targets

Technology: Preparing for tasks: Level B

Welsh PoS

Skills: Designing: 1, 2, 3, 4
Skills: Making: 8, 9

Background

Designing with food is often initially paper based. However, students should not start with a blank piece of paper. Designing with food needs an appreciation of the different factors involved, such as understanding ingredients, the application of healthy eating and nutrition, reflecting cultural and user needs, as well as organoleptic qualities. This unit highlights ways in which students can design better and more meaningful briefs based on good prior food experiences through simple ways of generating ideas.

Starter activity

Generate a class discussion by using the Resource sheet, 'Where do ideas come from?'. Students are to consider the ideas listed on the sheet: which of them have they experience of? Can they add to the list? Ask students to explain how these strategies could help them become more creative in their food design work.

Resource sheets and Activity sheets

The Activity sheet, 'Brief understanding', explains the concept of a design brief and requires students to read and interpret a set brief on a luxury scone product. Students might find it useful to use a dictionary or thesaurus during this task. Encourage students to share their ideas with the rest of the class on completion of the task. This activity could be extended by students actually making their scones.

The Activity sheet, 'Specification', explains the concept of a product specification and requires students to create their own specification. This requires them to record the type and amount of ingredients, how they are to be prepared, the method of making the product and what the final product should look like. Students should use this sheet when making their dish to check their specification was correct.

The Activity sheet, 'Ideas generator', provides a simple way of helping students generate ideas for their design by randomly choosing aspects of appearance, flavour and texture. Students are to randomly select a three digit number (from 000 to 999) and then use the details in a chart that correspond with the three numbers they have chosen.

The Activity sheet, 'Blank ideas generator', encourages students to develop their own suggestions for an ideas generator chart. They need to identify three food characteristics or attributes, followed by ten ideas for each of the three characteristics or attributes. Students should then choose a random three digit number (from 000 to 999) to select three of these items to develop their product from.

Plenary

Allow students to practise and apply the strategies for finding ideas listed on the Resource sheet, 'Where do ideas come from?', as well as provide plenty of opportunities for them to explore, evaluate and taste foods – a hands-on approach to food preparation and cooking plays a pivotal role in the development and design process of this subject.

Where do ideas come from?

Focusing on healthy eating

Being inspired by magazines and books

Evaluating and tasting new food dishes and recipes

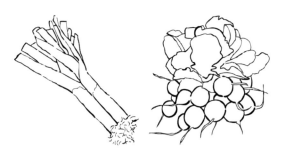
Using seasonal foods

Taking inspiration from other cultures

Using the Internet

Cooking at home

Visiting other countries

Talking to people about their favourite foods

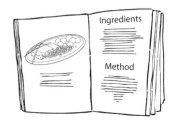
Reading recipe books

Calculating the cost of food

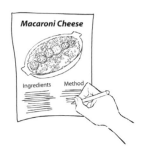
Modifying a recipe

Finding out about local foods

Activity sheet – Creativity

Brief understanding

A design **brief** provides clues to help you be creative and design a product to meet someone's needs or a particular purpose.

> ## Scone brief
>
> Design and make a novel luxury scone product for a family to share in the afternoon.

☞ 1 Underline the seven most important words in the brief that give clues about what you need to consider when designing your product. Write them in the table.

☞ 2 Next to each of the words, list other words, ideas or images you associate with them. You could use the ideas box to help you.

	Clues	Associated words, ideas and images
1		
2		
3		
4		
5		
6		
7		

Ideas box

- Create
- Craft
- New
- Exciting
- Innovative
- Posh
- Expensive
- Quality
- Traditional
- Object
- Creation
- Group
- People
- Split
- Divide
- Carve up
- Eating
- Occasion
- Tea
- Flavours

☞ 3 Design your final idea.

Specification

A product **specification** is a list of design criteria. When designing with food, the specification is similar to a recipe.

A product specification for food will include:

- Who it's for
- The type of ingredients to be used
- How the product should be made (method)
- The amount of ingredients to be used
- When/where it will be consumed
- How the ingredients should be prepared
- What the final product should look like

☞ Create your own product specification below.

Product name: _____		
Name of ingredients	**Quantity** **(for example, g, ml)**	**Preparation** **(for example, grated,** **chopped)**

Method

Details of final appearance (size, thickness, shape, decoration)

Ideas generator

The ideas generator will help generate lots of ideas for new food products!

☞ 1 Think of a three digit number between 000 and 999.

☞ 2 Compare your numbers against the chart below. Use the numbers to generate ideas for your product's appearance, flavour and texture.

For example, using the number 364 means the product will have a **smooth** appearance (3), a **fruity** flavour (6) and a **nutty** texture (4).

Number	Appearance	Flavour	Texture
0	Crunchy	Spicy	Smooth
1	Blended	Lemon	Crunchy
2	Crispy	Cheese	Soft
3	Smooth	Chocolate	Tangy
4	Wobbly	Garlic	Nutty
5	Bright	Ginger	Crispy
6	Moist	Fruity	Moist
7	Layered	Fish	Chewy
8	Soft	Beef	Juicy
9	Swirled	Vegetable	Sticky

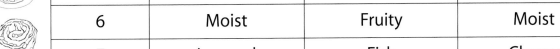

☞ 3 Fill in the spaces below to show what your product is going to be like.

My product is going to have a _____ appearance, a _____ flavour and a _____ texture.

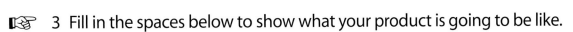
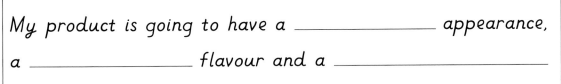
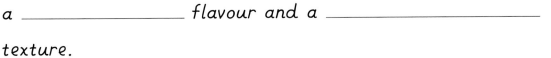

Activity sheet – Creativity

Blank ideas generator

The blank ideas generator will help you generate even more ideas for new food products!

☞ 1 Write down three food characteristics as headings. Write ten words under each of the headings that describe each of the characteristics. Use the ideas box to help.

Number	Characteristic 1 _____	Characteristic 2 _____	Characteristic 3 _____
0			
1			
2			
3			
4			
5			
6			
7			
8			
9			

Ideas box

- Appearance
- Country
- Smell
- Culture
- Shape
- Healthy eating
- Products
- Flavour
- Size
- Ingredients
- Texture
- Foods

☞ 2 Think of a three digit number and use it to come up with more food ideas.

Teacher's notes

The role of ingredients

Objectives

- To understand that foods and ingredients change during the cooking process
- To know the effect of heat on a range of ingredients
- To know which ingredients make food rise

Prior knowledge

Students should know that specific ingredients, in the correct proportions, are needed to produce a dish with a good quality finish.

NC links

Key concepts: 1.1 Designing and making; 1.2 Cultural understanding; 1.3 Creativity; 1.4 Critical evaluation
Key processes: e, f, g
Range and content: a, e, f, g, i
Curriculum opportunities: a

Northern Ireland PoS

Home economics: skills

Scottish attainment targets

Technology: Resources and how they are managed: Level C

Welsh PoS

Skills: Making: 1, 2, 6, 7, 8

Background

In this unit students will explore how ingredients change during cooking. This will develop an understanding of physical and chemical changes as well as the properties of the ingredients. Students will carry out four practical tasks which will familiarize them with the following changes: combining wet and dry ingredients, applying heat to ingredients using the microwave, hob and oven, and chemical changes when using baking powder as a raising agent.

Starter activity

Fill ice cube trays or lollipop moulds with pure fruit juice and freeze them. Give students a sample of the frozen juice and the juice at room temperature and ask them to explain why the two samples are different. Discuss with students how food can change when it is very hot or very cold.

Resource sheets and Activity sheets

The Activity sheet, 'The role of ingredients', lists ingredients and food dishes. Students are to identify which ingredient plays an important role in a specific dish. An alternative to students drawing arrows to link the items is to cut out and stick the correct images together in their workbooks as a resource.

The Activity sheet, 'Scrambled egg on toast', requires students to make scrambled egg on toast to appreciate the changes that happen to the ingredients. Students should highlight the effect of heat, the colour and texture change to bread, melted butter and the setting of egg. Ensure students use all cooking equipment safely.

The Activity sheet, 'Fruit muffins', requires students to make fruit muffins to appreciate the changes that happen to the ingredients. Students should highlight changes to both wet and dry ingredients when they are combined. Stress the role of baking powder and self-raising flour (help to make the muffins rise). The liquid in the batter forms steam which also aids rising.

The Activity sheet, 'Macaroni cheese', requires students to make macaroni cheese to appreciate the changes that happen to the ingredients. Students should highlight the effect of heat and water on the texture of the macaroni as it is cooked, the role of flour as a thickening agent in the sauce (flour absorbs liquid and swells when heated) and how the cheese melts and changes colour when heated under the grill.

The Activity sheet, 'Pasties', requires students to make a pasty to appreciate the changes that happen to the ingredients. Students should highlight the effect of water binding together flour, butter and egg (egg also forms a shiny glaze on the pastry when cooked). They should note changes in colour and texture to the mixture and the final product.

Plenary

As a class, recap on the changes that students have observed when cooking. Discuss the effect of heat on foods.

The role of ingredients

All ingredients play different roles in producing a final dish.

☞ The images on the left are ingredients. The images on the right are final dishes. Draw a line that matches each ingredient to a dish to show what role it plays in producing it.

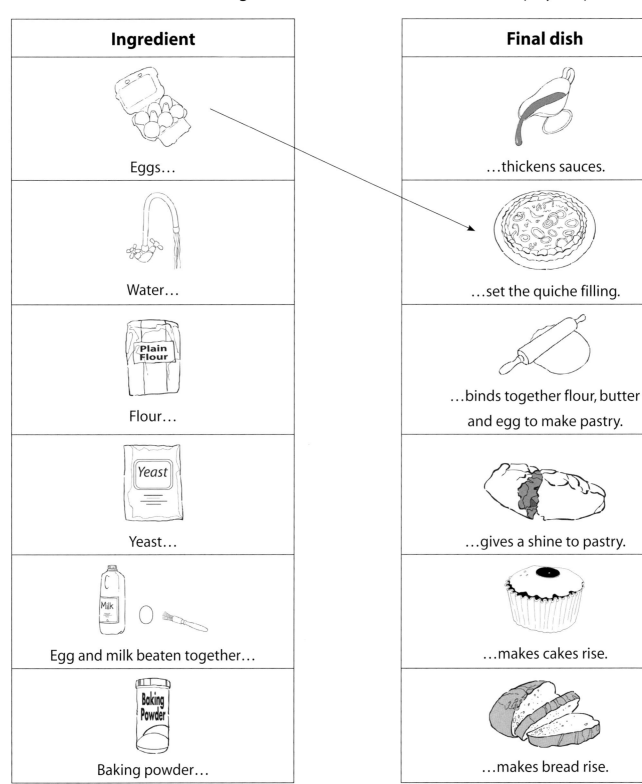

Ingredient	Final dish
Eggs…	…thickens sauces.
Water…	…set the quiche filling.
Flour…	…binds together flour, butter and egg to make pastry.
Yeast…	…gives a shine to pastry.
Egg and milk beaten together…	…makes cakes rise.
Baking powder…	…makes bread rise.

Activity sheet – The role of ingredients

Scrambled egg on toast

☞ Make scrambled egg on toast. Explain how the ingredients change. Use the ideas bank to help you.

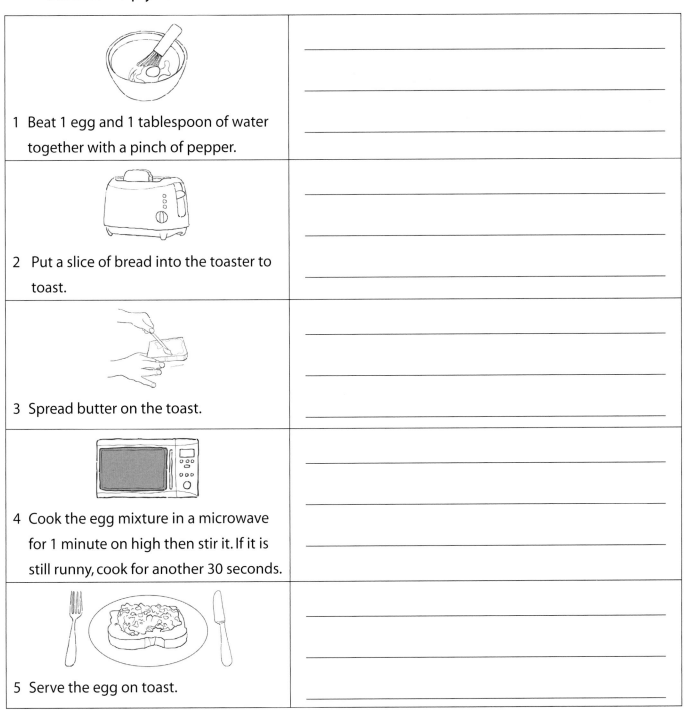

1 Beat 1 egg and 1 tablespoon of water together with a pinch of pepper.	
2 Put a slice of bread into the toaster to toast.	
3 Spread butter on the toast.	
4 Cook the egg mixture in a microwave for 1 minute on high then stir it. If it is still runny, cook for another 30 seconds.	
5 Serve the egg on toast.	

Ideas bank

- Liquid
- Pale yellow
- Sets
- Melts
- Hard
- Dark brown
- Dark yellow
- Crispy
- Soft
- Pale brown
- Crunchy

Activity sheet – The role of ingredients

Fruit muffins

☞ Make fruit muffins. Explain how the ingredients change. Use the ideas bank to help you.

1 Sieve the following ingredients into a mixing bowl: ● 250g white self-raising flour ● 2 x 5ml spoon baking powder 2 Stir in: ● 100g sugar ● 150g chopped fruit (fresh or dried)	_____
3 In a measuring jug, beat together: ● 2 eggs ● 250ml milk ● 80ml oil	_____
4 Pour the liquid ingredients into the dry ingredients. Stir until **just combined**. Spoon into 12 muffin cases. Bake at 190°C (gas mark 5) for 15–18 minutes.	_____
5 Place muffins on a cooling tray.	_____

Ideas bank

● Dry	● Thick	● Runny	● Golden brown	● Liquid
● Lumpy	● Wet	● Spongy	● Smooth	● Risen

Activity sheet – The role of ingredients

Macaroni cheese

☞ Make macaroni cheese. Explain how the ingredients change. Use the ideas bank to help you.

1 Put 100g macaroni and 1 litre of water in a large bowl. Cover the bowl with cling film. Make holes in the cling film and microwave on high for 20 minutes, or until al dente. 	_____ _____ _____ _____
2 In another bowl, blend together: ● 1 x 15ml spoon cornflour ● 250ml milk ● 1 x 2.5ml spoon mustard Bring to the boil, **stirring all the time**. Add 100g of grated cheese. 	_____ _____ _____ _____ _____ _____
3 Drain the macaroni and mix with the cheese sauce. Place the mixture into a greased serving dish. Sprinkle with grated cheese and arrange a sliced tomato on the top. Place under the grill until golden brown.	_____ _____ _____ _____ _____

Ideas bank

● Hard   ● Runny   ● Soft   ● The cheese melts

● Golden brown   ● The flour thickens the sauce   ● Smooth

Activity sheet – The role of ingredients

Pasties

☞ Make a pasty. Explain how the ingredients change. Use the ideas bank to help you.

1 Sieve 100g of plain flour into a bowl. Rub in 50g of margarine. Bind together with 2 or 3 15ml measures of cold water. 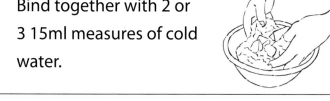	_____ _____ _____ _____
2 In another bowl mix together: ● 100g grated cheese ● 3 finely chopped spring onions ● 25g peas, mushrooms or beans ● ½ small egg, beaten ● Pinch of pepper 	_____ _____ _____ _____
3 Roll out the pastry and cut out a circle or square. Fill the shape with cheese mixture. Stick the pastry edges together with water. Place the pastry on a greased baking sheet. Brush the pastry with the remaining ½ of the beaten egg. Bake at 190°C (gas mark 5) for 20–25 minutes. 	_____ _____ _____ _____ _____ _____ _____

Ideas bank

● Dry	● Hard	● Smooth	● Crispy	● Bind together
● Set	● Golden brown	● Moist	● Soft	

Teacher's notes

Recipe challenge

Objectives

- To understand the necessity of a healthy diet
- To select healthy ingredients for recipes
- To adapt recipes by adding or substituting ingredients using healthier options

Prior knowledge

Students should know the names of food groups and be aware that food provides nutrients that are essential to the functioning of their bodies.

NC links

Key concepts: 1.1 Designing and making;
1.3 Creativity
Key processes: c, e
Range and content: a, f, h
Curriculum opportunities: a, b, c, d, e, f, g

Northern Ireland PoS

Home economics: Diet and health: a, b
Technology and design: Designing: d, g

Scottish attainment targets

Technology: Resources and how they are managed: Level B
Processes and how they are applied: Level A

Welsh PoS

Skills: Designing: 3, 4, 5, 8, 9
Skills: Making: 1, 2, 6, 7, 9

Background

This unit aims to stimulate students' understanding of how they can adapt recipes and eating habits to promote a healthy but appetizing dish. There are four recipe challenges that focus on how to cook with more fibre, less saturated fat, less salt and reduced sugar.

Starter activity

Refer back to the Resource sheet, 'The eatwell plate', to remind students about different food groups. Promote a discussion about why students think the sections of the plate are different sizes and if they should think about how much food they eat from each section every day.

Resource sheets and Activity sheets

The Resource sheet, 'Take the healthy option', provides students with five statements that promote ways of healthier eating. As a class discuss the following ideas: use wholemeal ingredients to increase fibre intake, use low-fat ingredients, use vegetable oils instead of animal fat, use herbs and spices as a whole or partial substitute to salt, use fresh or dried fruit to add sweetness instead of sugar or to reduce the amount of sugar used.

The Activity sheet, 'Milkshake challenge', encourages students to think about alternative, healthier ingredient options. Discuss how and why each ingredient could be substituted. Providing students with the suggested healthy-option foods would add interest and inspiration for them to adapt the recipe. The focus of this sheet is a low-fat product with a high fruit content.

The Activity sheet, 'Sandwich challenge', requires students to look at (and perhaps sample) a range of ways of creating a sandwich to make it healthier. Students should be encouraged to choose breads that are high in fibre and healthy-option fillings.

The Activity sheet, 'Dessert challenge', requires students to suggest healthy options to create a chilled, layered dessert. Encourage students to include fresh, canned or frozen fruit in their dessert as well as low-fat and low-sugar ingredients.

The Activity sheet, 'Burger challenge', provides a recipe for burgers. Students need to adapt the recipe to reduce its fat and salt content. Students should be encouraged to think about a healthier bread roll option (such as wholemeal) and include vegetables as extras. A visit to a place that sells burgers would stimulate interest and add authenticity to the challenge.

Plenary

As a class or in small groups students could evaluate the results of each of the challenges by deciding if they have chosen the healthiest alternatives and if their final dishes looked and tasted good.

Take the healthy option

Base your meals on starchy foods.

Cut down on saturated fat.

Eat lots of fruit and vegetables.

Try to eat less salt (no more than six grams a day).

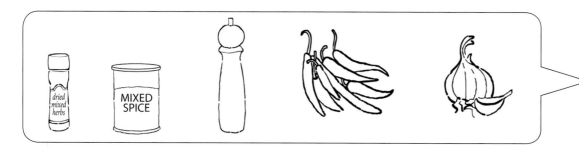

Cut down on sugar.

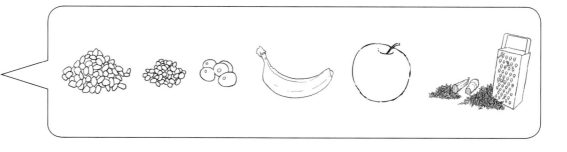

Milkshake challenge

The following instructions show you how
to make a traditional milkshake.

Healthy
hints!

Blend or whisk together:

- *300ml milk*
- *4 x 5ml spoons of milkshake powder*
- *1 dessert spoon of ice cream*

Low
fat

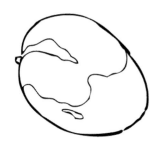

Use fresh,
frozen or canned
fruit

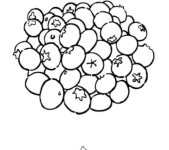

👉 1 Suggest three ways in which the milkshake could be made healthier.

1 _____

2 _____

3 _____

👉 2 Make a milkshake using your healthy suggestions.

Food 2

Activity sheet – Recipe challenge

Sandwich challenge

☞ Make a ham sandwich. Explain how you could change the ingredients to make it a healthier sandwich. Use the ideas about bread, fillings and extras to help you.

Panini

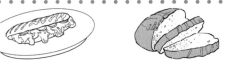
Wholemeal bread

Milk roll

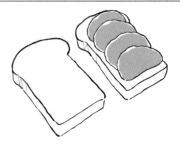
Seeded bread

1 Spread butter on two slices of bread.

2 Put ham on one of the slices of bread.

3 Cover the ham covered slice of bread with the second slice of bread. Cut it into two or four pieces. To make a toasted sandwich, place the sandwich under the grill.

Bread: _____

Fillings: _____

_____

Extras: _____

_____

Fillings

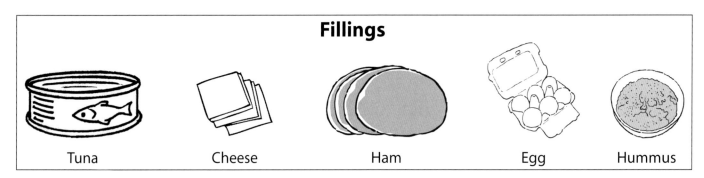

Tuna   Cheese   Ham   Egg   Hummus

Extras

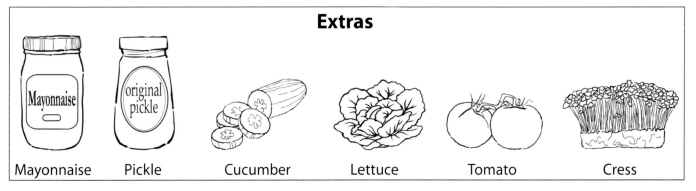

Mayonnaise   Pickle   Cucumber   Lettuce   Tomato   Cress

Activity sheet – Recipe challenge

Dessert challenge

☞ 1 How can you change the chilled, layered dessert? Use the word bank to help you.

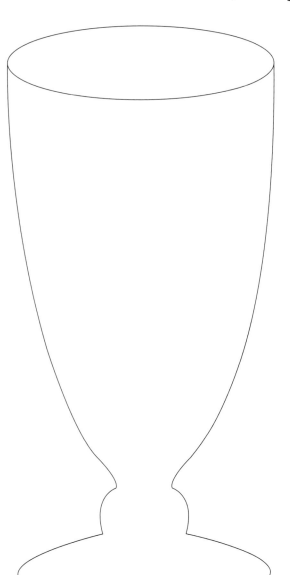

Instead of a glacé cherry, use: _____

Instead of double cream, use: _____

Instead of marshmallows, use: _____

Instead of strawberry mousse, use: _____

Instead of Swiss roll, use: _____

☞ 2 Design a new dessert and label each item. Try to make it with less fat, less sugar and more fruit.

Word bank

Strawberries

Strawberry yogurt

Banana

Natural yogurt

Sugar-free jelly

Low-fat custard

_____

_____

_____

_____

Burger challenge

☞ 1 Make a burger. How could you reduce the fat and salt content of the burger recipe?

1 Mix together the following ingredients: • 200g minced meat • 1 x 5ml spoon of salt • 1 x 1.25ml spoon of pepper	**Reduce the fat by:** _____ _____ _____ _____
2 Divide the mixture in two and shape them into burgers. Brush each burger with oil and cook in the oven at 190°C (gas mark 5) for 20 minutes.	**Reduce the salt by:** _____ _____ _____ _____

Word bank

• Lean minced beef   • Spray oil   • Herbs   • Spices   • Garlic

☞ 2 Design your burger in a bun. Try to think of ways of adding fibre. Use the ideas bank to help you. Label your diagram.

_____   _____

_____   _____

_____   _____

Ideas bank

• Lettuce   • Tomato   • Gherkins   • Onion   • Low-fat mayonnaise   • Ketchup

Teacher's notes

Tasting and testing

Objectives

- To use a variety of sensory vocabulary when describing food
- To taste and test raw food and prepared dishes
- To critically assess their own and their peers' products

Prior knowledge

Students should already be aware that ingredients and food products have a variety of sensory characteristics and that people have different likes and dislikes, which affect their evaluation of food.

NC links

Key concepts: 1.4 Critical evaluation
Key processes: h
Range and content: a, i
Curriculum opportunities: a

Northern Ireland PoS

Home economics: skills
Technology and design: Designing: f, h

Scottish attainment targets

Technology: Resources and how they are managed:
Level A

Welsh PoS

Skills: Designing: 8, 9
Skills: Making: 9

Background

This unit provides students with a range of vocabulary to use when tasting and testing food, and by carrying out preference and discrimination tests. Preference tests give information about people's likes and dislikes and are subjective. Discrimination tests aim to evaluate specific attributes and are objective. Testing enables students to evaluate food and suggest improvements.

Starter activity

Provide students with samples of different foods such as an orange, a chocolate drop and a Hula Hoop so that they can look at, feel and taste them. Students should note that they are all round in shape but have different tastes and textures. Discuss with students what particular characteristics they think each item has in relation to its appearance, texture and taste (round, salty, sweet, dry, and so on). Discuss which senses are being used when evaluating these characteristics (sight, smell, taste and touch).

Resource sheets and Activity sheets

The Resource sheet, 'Attribute words', provides a range of descriptive words about food. It could be used as a way of extending the starter activity by providing students with more characteristic examples or could be enlarged and laminated to be used as a display for students to refer to.

The Activity sheet, 'Ranking food', requires students to taste and evaluate a number of different fruits in relation to specific attributes. Each attribute should be explained to students beforehand. This Activity sheet could be used as a template, with the range of foods and attributes changed as required.

The Activity sheet, 'Comparing food products', requires students to record information about people's likes and dislikes of different or similar foods. This is a subjective test. To enable fair results, food should be placed in containers and numbered. The tests should be undertaken in an area with no distractions and the results recorded immediately. Provide water to clean the palate between each tasting.

The Activity sheet, 'Sensory evaluation', requires students to use a star chart to record sensory attributes of a food product. Students are to choose six different attributes that describe a product. They must test the product and decide the intensity of each attribute by numbering them 0 to 5 (5 being the highest). Students are to record each score on the star chart and then analyse their results.

Plenary

As a class, review the different methods of testing products to decide which one was most effective, based on ease-of-use and effectiveness of outcome.

Resource sheet – Tasting and testing

Attribute words

risen **Round** *Attractive* Square *Flat*

Golden Brown

Colourful

Looks

Crispy Moist

Juicy Soft DRY CHEWY

Crunchy

Texture

spicy **SALTY** savoury *Sour*

Bland sweet Peppery

BITTER *Fruity*

Taste and smell

Activity sheet – Tasting and testing

Ranking food

☞ 1 Taste the foods that are shown below. Give each item a score from 1 to 4 for each of the attributes given. A score of 4 means it is the crunchiest, sweetest or juciest.

Food	Crunchy	Sweet	Juicy

☞ 2 Based on your results from Task 1, answer the following questions.

a Which food is the most crunchy? _____

b Which food is the most sweet? _____

c Which food is the most juicey? _____

Activity sheet – Tasting and testing

Comparing food products

☞ 1 Put a sample of each food to be tested in similar containers – one for each person taking part.

☞ 2 Number each sample. Remember to keep a record of the numbers!

☞ 3 In a quiet area, test each sample and fill in the chart below. Remember to drink water between tasting each sample.

Food sample	Poor 🙁	Average 😐	Good 🙂
1			
2			
3			
4			
5			
6			

☞ 4 Once you have finished, answer the questions below.

   a Which food had the poorest taste? _____

   b Which food had an average taste? _____

   c Which food had the best taste? _____

Activity sheet – Tasting and testing

Sensory evaluation

☞ 1 On the star chart write six different attribute words to describe a food product.

Name of product: _____

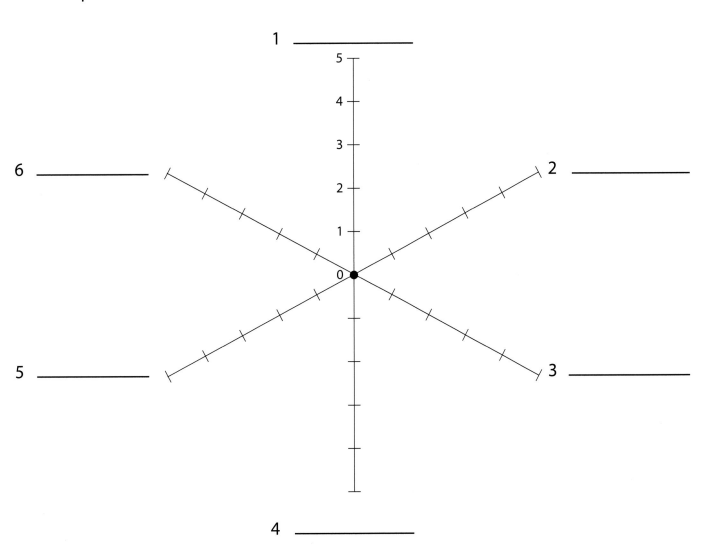

☞ 2 Taste your product and give it a mark from 0 to 5 for each attribute. Fill in the star chart.

☞ 3 Answer the following questions:

    a The product had a high score for: _____

    b The product had a low score for: _____

    c I could improve the product by: _____

_____

Assessment sheet – Food 2

Self-assessment

Name of dish: _____

My dish looks _____.

My dish tastes _____.

The texture of my dish is _____.

I could improve my dish by _____

_____.

Peer-assessment

Your dish looks _____.

You could improve your dish by _____

_____.

Teacher assessment